ARTIFICIAL INTELLIGENCE

MAN VS MACHINE: BEGINNING OR THE END

A Word !

Westworld, TV series attained maximum ratings for its last aired series. The series have raised serious questions about AI through its plot. The creator of the artificial world where AI machines were being used to mimic real life thought that he could control the level of growth of AI machines, but AI machines managed to raise their ingenuity that ultimately went out of hand of humans.

The topic is not new nor is considered so much taboo. The 2004 film I, Robot touched the same tunes.

The self driving cars, drones and robots are not a myth anymore. Taking lead from advancements in AI in civil sector, militaries round the globe have implemented AI for surveillance, Air defence systems, cyber security, missile defence system etc. The command and control system of weapon systems in militaries is being heavily impacted by use of AI in sensor and data analysis system. However, AI is not without its limitations and implications. The effect of errors and manipulation of AI systems can create a havoc especially when used in nuclear weapons control systems. History has very solid examples where automation systems failed, and only human intervention saved the day. The book is an effort to discuss the impacts of Artificial intelligence on command and control systems and how far we are willing to go to forego human control especially at sensitive locations.

ABOUT THE AUTHOR

Hassan is a Telecommunication Engineer by profession with Bachelor of Engineering in Telecommunications and Masters in Computer Science. He also holds multiple Certifications in Computer Networking and Network Security from Huawei, Cisco and Microsoft.

Visit the official Authors Website

http://ammarhassan.me/

One More Thing

If you Like the book or if you have any suggestions, do comment, and provide feedback. Thanks!

Happy Reading !

Table Of Contents

CHAPTER 1

INTRODUCTION

Artificial intelligence (AI), a concept which originated in 1956, is now a reality in the lives of most people. Recent advancements in algorithms combined with an explosion in the amount of data available have paved the way for a wide variety of uses of AI that are likely to have far-reaching effects not just on our economies and the way we work, but also in the world strategic balances.

Artificial Intelligence (AI) refers to the self-learning programs that may replace a human job completely through context based, patterns based & recognition-based learning. To state in simple terms, **"AI is software that has the capability to observe and learn from human data in order to mimic human behaviour/ responses".** More specifically, Artificial intelligence is used in applications which aim to:

1. Detect and recognize data (text, voice, images, video etc.) or predict future data.

2. Seek correlations between data to deduce a generic form of behaviour from them or flag up ab-

normal behaviour.

3. Optimize highly combinational problems such as logistical processes or flight routes.

4. Reasoning from symbolic data to deduce or diagnose.

Advances in the last decade, such as massive data processing algorithms using deep neural networks, increased computing power, and the use of graphics processing units (GPUs) have caused a ripple effect, resulting in the discovery of new efficient AI techniques. These effects have been amplified by sharing open-source algorithms and by research collaborations. Despite this undeniable progress however, AI technologies are still far from robust in unknown environments that are difficult to generalize. Their results can sometimes be hard to explain or lead to gross errors. This explains why most AI applications today remain limited to elementary or non-critical tasks. In the defence sphere, AI technologies will have to make further progress before they can be used in a controlled way.

Artificial intelligence (AI), particularly the fields of machine learning (ML) and deep learning (DL), has evolved from prototyping in research institutes and universities to actual applications for the deployment in the actual world. The performance of artificial intelligence applications such as "machine translation, QA systems and speech recognition" has been revolutionized with constant efforts of academia. The advancement in AI research fields have also turned other imaginative ideas into

notable AI applications that include video synthesis, photo analysis, automatic control systems, battlefield awareness and speech mimicking etc.

While the public may have been impressed by the success of Alphago or the sporting prowess of Boston Dynamics' robots, AI is still not widely used in practical industrial and commercial applications. Quickest to take up these burgeoning new technologies have been the e-commerce, marketing, industrial maintenance, and human resources sectors. For private individuals, the first applications to use unstructured data such as speech and image processing are intruding home speakers and smartphones. In the health sector, very significant progress has been made in tumour image analysis, achieving higher levels of recognition than even the most experienced professionals.

Most of these achievements stem from major digital players, especially American and Chinese, which have access to what really fuels AI: the vast mass of data that their customers provide to them free of charge at each interaction. Having initially sought to know their customers better to enhance their products and services, these actors are now using their deep pockets to pursue greater ambitions, such as driverless cars, smart cities and personalized healthcare. Their products set the standard, and the sheer extent of their use cases makes them attractive to the military, especially in the many dual- use applications.

Some see AI as a great source of progress for

humanity, relieving people of tedious tasks and increase their cognitive capacities while improving their health and access to knowledge. Others only perceive the threats that AI already poses to our democracies and our privacy and could pose in the future to our ethical values. Artificial intelligence has the potential to transform health care, agriculture, and business logistics sector that are the key drives for human development.

Between immortality, trans humanism and the end of the world heralded by the reign of robots, artificial intelligence is the nexus of all hopes and fears and, in some cases, it is also becoming a focus of fierce global competition. Almost every week, major powers, private companies, some of them with very substantial economic clout, announce new breakthroughs and massive new investment in AI. This book focuses on finding answers to major questions that come in our mind whenever we hear the term AI, especially in Nuclear and strategic weapons domain.

CHAPTER-2

DEMYSTIFYING AI

The artificial intelligence (AI) has gained increased attention from multiple sources, including both media and political community over the years. The misconception about an actual understanding of AI remains unsolved, despite many publications and seminars on this topic. There are in fact increased concerns now about the capability of AI systems and how dangerous they can be. Most of the confusions are created due to the exaggerated portrayal of AI in mainstream science and fiction genre of the media.

Although this section of computer science has been in the limelight for more than a decade, the misconceptions however are now being amplified more due to the noticeable progress of computer science in the last few years. AI being the hot topic for media persons is misused to create flashy headline tickers exaggerating what all it can accomplish and damage it can cause. Since the exaggerated version gains more hype, the actual risks and opportunities linked with AI get neglected and the true capabilities and threats of AI technology remain untouched.

Alan Turing in 1950 wrote the paper **"Computing Machinery and Intelligence"**. The paper starts with the questions **"I propose to consider the question: Can machines think?"** This led scientists to consider if building an electronic brain is possible. This was a quantum jump from hardware thinking to software solutions. The word AI was coined by "John McCarthy, an American computer scientist, in 1956 at The Dartmouth Conference" and AI as discipline was born. Attendees became the forefathers of AI research. Herbert Simon predicted, "Machines will be capable, within twenty years of doing any work a man can do". Timeline for the evolution of AI is briefly explained as under:

1950 – Turing Test.   Computer scientist Alan Turing proposed a simple test for assessing machine intelligence. "If a machine can trick humans into thinking it is human, then it has intelligence."

1955 – Coining of AI.   Term 'Artificial Intelligence' was coined by computer scientist, John McCarthy and he described AI as "the science and engineering of making intelligent machines".

1961 – Unimate.   Unimate was the first industrial robot that replaced humans on the assembly line at General Motors.

1964 – Eliza.   Eliza was the Ground breaking chatbot which was developed by Joseph Weizenbaum at MIT and could converse with humans.

1966 – Shakey. The 'first electronic person' from Stanford, Shakey was created as a "the first electronic person". The robot could reason about its actions and decisions.

1997 – Deep Blue. 1997, saw a robot called Deep Blue, defeating a world chess champion, Garry Kasparov.

1998 – Kismet. Cynthia Breazeal at MIT created Kismet, "an emotionally intelligent robot that recognizes and reacts to people's feelings".

1999 – AiBO. Sony commercially launched the first consumer robot pet dog AiBO (AI robot). The robot could develop skills and personality over time.

2002 – ROOMBA. The first mass commercially available autonomous robotic vacuum cleaner was created that could learn to navigate and clean homes in an efficient way.

2011 – SIRI and Watson. Apple introduces Siri, a virtual assistant with a voice interface, and integrated it into the iPhone 4S. The same year, IBM's Watson computer won the first prize in the popular $1 million television quiz show "Jeopardy".

2014 – Eugene and Alexa. Eugene Goostman, a chatbot fooled one-third of the judges believing that Eugene is human and passed Turing test. The same year, Amazon launched a smart virtual assistant with a voice interface called "Alexa" that revolutionized smart shopping.

2017 – Alphago. Google's A.I. AlphaGo defeated the world champion Ke Jie in the board game of Go. The game is known to be one of the most complex games having a number of (2*170) possible positions.

AI has affected nearly all walks of our life. The

major applications where effect is prominent and sufficient gains have been achieved are as follows:-

Digital Assistants

Digital assistants like Apple's Siri, Google Now, Amazon's Alexa, and Microsoft's Cortana help users to perform various routine tasks. These virtual assistants help people in checking daily schedules and searching specifics on the web. They also provide an interface to control other applications by sending different commands. They work efficiently as they learn from every user interaction and keep on assessing user habits. Digital voice assistants are fast becoming our daily partners and we are developing habits of taking assistance from them in getting route directions to the hotels to asking about the current temperature and forecasts for the weekends. These assistants use natural language processing and AI-techniques to return the answers.

Web Searches

The usage of a search engine is not new. It has been in use since the 90s. The frequency of use of search engines varies with different age groups. However, it is only recently that the entire search experience on the web has been transformed with introduction of AI.

The highlight feature of AI in improving the search experience is the development of smart ranking algorithms. Although human effort has been put in designing and tuning of these algorithms, the search engines however use artificial intelligence techniques to further improve their functionality.

By doing this, the quality of smart search on the engines has increased remarkably.

Another key role played by artificial intelligence techniques is in quality control. Many wrong methods have been implemented by desperate marketers around the world to improve their search ranking which includes: the practice of keyboard stuffing and invisible text. The penalizing of such practices by websites is now easily done by AI. Hence, they keep the poor credibility pages out of the top search results.

Manufacturing and Production

The application of AI systems in the industrial sector helps the manufacturers in maintaining the quality control. Automated smart systems can do proactive monitoring and data analysis that in turn enables preventive or predictive maintenance. AI technologies improve the efficiency of production cycles by making them less time consuming. Such automation is termed robotic process automation (RPA).

Robots

Over the years, the emerging field of Robotics has gained much hype and Artificial intelligence (AI) is arguably the most exciting area in robotics. It has been agreed by all that robot can work on the assembly line, but its intelligence remains questionable to date.

Like the term "robot" itself, artificial intelligence, is difficult to define. The ultimate version of AI seems unattainable yet as it requires replica of the human thought process and intellect. Robots still have a long way to go in achieving this supreme goal, but they have achieved considerable milestones. Today AI machines can emulate few elements of intellectual abilities if not all abilities required to learn, reason, and formulate ideas.

The learning capacity of robots is still quite limited. Learning robots make generic rules by recognizing the actions that achieved the desired results. A record of successful actions is kept applying when a certain scenario occurs. Again, modern computers can only do this in very limited situations. A robot still cannot take in information like a human can. Some robots now can also interact socially. Kismet, a robot at MT's Artificial Intelligence Laboratory, recognizes human body language and voice inflexion by use of sensors and responds appropriately. The low-level interaction between babies and humans based solely on the tone of speech is considered as the basis for design of Kismet human-like learning system.

Games

AI in games enables the use of smart problem solving and learning skills to acquire appropriate performance levels. AI is used to acknowledging the structured collection of rules for games such as chess and go scrabble, and then turning them into frameworks that can be used to develop abilities. AI introduces the element of unpredictability to games, making them more interesting else people would have lost interest in it. The game industry was possibly one of the first to adopt artificial intelligence. Every game you play has an AI feature in it, in some form or another. When you enjoy a game like "CS: GO," "PUBG," or "Fortnite," you will almost always start with a few AI-powered bots before moving on to real players. Furthermore, if you are playing a single-player game, you will always be pitted against AI bots.

Streaming Services

Music and movies delivery platforms, which we all use regularly, are another excellent example of how AI is affecting our daily lives. AI makes choices for you whether you use Soundcloud, Netflix, or YouTube. These services log your searches and even recommend a playlist that suits your tastes. Doesn't it get scarier, they know you better than you like?

Smartphones

Smartphones today stand out as the most crucial technological product that we own. AI has been implemented subtly in many ways to make the phones smarter. The predictive text feature suggests all possible words that can be used to complete the sentences typed. Almost all applications on the phone are implementing AI features in one way or the other. A specific search on any one platform makes it easy for the various algorithms running to display similar results on all apps like Facebook, Instagram and twitter etc.

Smart Cars and Drones

Just a few years ago, driving a completely or even semi-automated vehicle was a pipe dream.

Companies like Tesla have advanced to the point that we now have a fleet of semi-automated vehicles on the route. Tesla automobiles are an excellent example of how artificial intelligence influences our everyday lives. All Tesla cars are related, and the information your car gathers is shared with the rest of the fleet. That ensures that after the update, if a car does an abrupt left turn at an intersection, all Tesla cars will know how to handle it.

"Unmanned Aerial Vehicles (UAVs)" or "Drones" are an essential part of our airspace. These are used not only as monitoring devices but also as a carrier in delivery services required for a growing number of systems. Some of such recent systems include the delivery of medicine and basic supplies to elderly citizens locked in their homes due to COVID-19.

Social Media

Most of the social media applications used by almost all age groups are AI-assisted. Most of user's decisions are affected by artificial intelligence. From the common news feeds, you see in your timeline to the notifications you get from these apps; everything is curated by AI. The entire experience of using such apps has been custom tailored. It takes all our past actions on such platforms, search history and all interactions to design a specific algorithm for you. The addition of smart algorithms in applications makes the entire experience so addictive for the users that they continuously revisit the apps.

Twitter. The use of Artificial intelligence is more backstage, a lot of data is processed using neural networks to evaluate the user preferences and record them for later use. The entire user experience of the app is improved from tweet recommendations to tackling inappropriate or racist content to improving the user experience.

Facebook. One of the important concepts of AI is deep learning based on the "torch framework". This is the very concept implemented in the much-famed social media app of Facebook. Deep learning is helping Facebook to extract meaningful information from the random unstructured data. Recently a socially responsible feature was added by Facebook's team of developers for proactive detection of pattern formed by user's posts indicating possibility of self-harm in the future. The smart AI-powered procedures deliver mental health services to the relevant authorities and his or her circle if a suspicious pattern is identified. Facebook provides human capital for this AI initiative, including certified moderators, collaborations with local mental health agencies, and, if necessary, local first responders.

Instagram. With the increased number of users on Instagram in recent years, this app is also using big data artificial intelligence to target advertising, to monitor cyberbullying and remove offensive comments. Artificial intelligence has facilitated the users to prioritize their information, manage spam posts and improve the overall user experience.

Chatbots

Customers with popular questions will get support from chatbots, which understand words and phrases and offer relevant content. Chatbots can be so precise that it is as though you're conversing with a human.

Online Industry

One industry that has flourished most from the addition of artificial intelligence is the online advertising industry. This industry not only uses AI procedures to keep track of user statistics but also published ads based on the data collected from those statistics. In today's busy world, time is money. No user is interested in wasting time on random useless advertisements. Smart algorithms gather useful data only and then suggest new products based on preferred choices.

Navigation and Travel

Another useful application of AI is in the Navigation services like Google / Apple Maps. Vehicle for hire companies like Careem / Uber taxi services also use AI. These navigation services use artificial intelligence algorithms to interpret the thousands of data points received and bring the real-time traffic data.

Deep learning, a branch of artificial intelligence, is used by cars with self-driving and automatic parking features to explore the environment around them. Nvidia is a technology firm that uses artificial intelligence to "give vehicles the ability to see, think, and understand so that they can drive through an almost unlimited number of potential driving scenarios."

Banking and Finance

With the advent of Internet banking, cyber-crime / fraud has multiplied. Fraud protection and customer service are the prime focus of the banking and finance industry. The simplest example is the automated emails and text messages you receive from banks on making logging into your accounts and after any transaction is being made. AI is also being trained to look at large samples of fraud data and find a pattern so that you can be noticed before it happens to you. Big players in the financial industry incorporate the smart methods of AI to analyse data and make informed investment decisions. Decisions that help them gain highest returns with least amount of risk involved are predicted by AI-assisted programs. If you scan a pay check with your phone to deposit it, you'll get a low balance warning or a reminder to log into your bank account online. Behind the scenes, AI is at work. If you go to a store for lunch and buy a new pair of jeans, artificial intelligence will verify the buying to see if it is a "normal" transaction and either validate or reject the transaction, fearing that your credit card is being used fraudulently.

Healthcare

AI is also empowering the machines used in health and life sciences. From diagnosis to analysis, from prediction of the course of various types of disease to monitoring patient's health conditions; AI is handling it all. AI systems and robotics are also facilitating the medical staff by taking physical workload off the medical personnel and automating many of the administrative and routine functions of health facilities.

Commercial Airline Flights

The advancement in the field of AI has led to the concept of automated flights. The actual manual flying duration of many flights these days is quite surprising. A survey in recent past of the airline's Boeing 777 pilots found that they only fly 7 minutes manually on a typical flight, with most of the task being done by AI technology. According to a report by Wired Magazine, Boeing is working to build jet-liners fully controlled by artificial intelligence - with no human pilots at the helm.

Email Communications

Smart Reply templates are commonly used in emails and business accounts to give users the ability to save time. Pre-tailored email replies with simple phrases like "Yes, I'm working on it". or "No, I haven't." are sent with just the click of a button. Smart replies are tailored to the content of each email. Users can respond by entering a manual answer or choose a smart answer with one click instead.

The inbox management system organizes emails and promotions in the most authentic manner. Emails are automatically sorted into categories. The program helps you organize your e-mails so that you can get to important communications faster.

Security and Surveillance

Involvement and impact of AI in security and

surveillance systems is undeniable. Simultaneous monitoring of huge number of monitors and camera is a tedious task and is also not feasible. With advance technologies like object recognition and face recognition getting better by the day, it won't be long before all security is analysed in automatic fashion. Camera feeds are monitored by an AI rather than a human. Drone surveillance, AI-based facial recognition, and biometric systems improve the security profiles of the organizations and governments that use them. While this is positive, there are of course concerns about privacy, espionage, and the "Big Brother" factor.

CHAPTER-3

Rise of AI Machines

In the past several decades, digital technology has undeniably altered the face of the planet. When computers were first developed, they were just used for numerical computations. However, as time passed and new technologies were invented, computers began to take over most of the skilled workers. This further developed into artificial intelligence (AI), which seeks to operate more intelligently than humans.

The acceleration of AI development in the last two decades thus has made it necessary to carefully research how to enable the inception of such technology robustly in order to prevent the catastrophic risk of its premature adoption in the near or distant future, especially concerning the appeal of its radical adoption through profit or power-oriented private and public international actors.

The pioneering cryptographer and computer scientist I.J. Good proclaimed in 1965 that: -

"The first ultra-intelligent machine is the last invention that man need ever make, provided that the machine is docile enough to tell us how to keep

it under control."

Smart vehicles, intelligent vacuums that can do automatic cleaning, studying home designs, and guns that can automatically strike a target, determining danger and take judgments without human interference are all examples of AI. AI is very difficult to define and even more difficult in military contexts. With the ever-increasing technology advancement in the modern warfare, Artificial intelligence (AI) has emerged as a crucial part of many defence systems. Compared to standard systems, military systems armed with AI can process and analyse huge data quantities with improved efficiency. Because of its built-in decision making and computing capabilities, AI improves many features of combat systems that include autonomous control, monitoring and activation. Major players of the world have already committed their resources to AI and are striving to own the data. The recent war of technologies between Huawei and USA is a recent example of this race.

Artificial intelligence can be interpreted in many ways and is used in multiple ways in military arena. AI is not a single technology, and therefore there are various ways in which it could be applied in the military field. For example, Russian Ministry of Defence is interested in **"combat robots"**. These robots are "multifunctional devices with anthropomorphic human-like behaviour that partially or fully perform functions of a person in carrying out a particular combat mission. This includes a sensor system for gathering information, a control system and actuation devices". AI can be used for combat robots or to analyse data and has the capability to reduce human involvement in risk based environments.

The pivot innovation of driver-less vehicles which are able to navigate street traffic, was initiated by the Pentagon's own research institution, the **Defence Advanced Research Projects Agency (DARPA)**, from 2004 to 2007 during a scientific challenge to develop any kind of unmanned vehicle able to move only an inch without human help.

Science Fiction movies and Tv Series like "I, Robot" and "Westworld" have also developed keep interest of people in AI driven robots and the extent of damage that we should expect in case AI goes rogue. The question of AI robots walking among humans has not been restricted to "if they Will", but it should now be considered as "when and how soon".

According to a recent Oxford and Yale University survey of over 350 AI researchers, machines are predicted to be better than us at translating languages by 2024, writing high-school essays by 2026, driving a truck by 2027, working in retail by 2031, writing a book by 2049 and surgery by 2053.

In his 2006 book The Singularity is Near, American author and futurist Ray Kurzweil predicted, among many other things, that AI will soon surpass humans. By 2099, he forecasted that machines would have attained equal legal status with humans, harking back to movies like the Bicentennial Man, starring the late Robin Williams, where a humanoid-turned-human is granted the status of a human by the courts. AI experts will tell us that no such thing is likely to happen in the near future. Nevertheless, given the rapid advancements in the technology, it is better to be safe than sorry.

CHAPTER-4

Militarization of AI

"Securing Our Common Future", A Strategy for Disarmament, released by UN Secretary-General Antonio Guterres in 2018, proposed a detailed disarmament agenda and related action plans. He also stressed the importance of coping with new warfare means and strategies, such as bringing arms and artificial intelligence under human influence.

"The concept of weapons control for AI persists in its infancy," wrote Kenneth Payne of King's College London in Survival, since "the advantages of possessing weaponized AI are likely to be profound and because there will be persistent problems in defining technologies and monitoring compliance."

These strategies focus on different areas, and include scientific research, talent development, skills and education, public and private sector adoption, ethics and inclusion, standards and regulations, and data and digital infrastructure. So, it seems that nations will "spar" over AI through competition in research, investment, and talent. Military application of AI is often compared to the use of electricity. As with using electricity, no country could be banned from using AI. Just as with the arms race between the United States and the Soviet Union during the Cold War, "an algorithm race between AI powers is likely to emerge in the future." But unlike the arms-control agreements reached between the United States and the Soviet Union at that time, such a consensus on an algorithm-control agreement is unlikely to materialize, given the current state of major power relations.

AI in Military applications has the potential to increase risks of war and can increase its lethality many folds. These new technologies are mostly being developed by the private sector and the same is being depicted in science fiction dramas and books. These emerging technologies are constantly presenting new challenges to governments and another major stakeholder.

The Stanley Centre for Peace and Security, in cooperation with the United Nations Office for Arms control Policies and the Stimson Center, written many articles co-authored by Paul Scharre, Vadim Kozyulin, and Wu Jinhuai to discuss the threats and analyse the implications of artificial intelligence militarization. Their essays offer "basic framework to direct readers and outline the challenges in identifying what artificial intelligence is and how artificial intelligence can influence the behaviour of war."

For national militaries, AI has wide potential that goes beyond weapon systems. AI applications are considered as the means for jobs that are "boring, dirty and dangerous". They provide a means of "avoiding human lives being put at risk or being assigned tasks that do not require the creativity of the human brain". AI systems also have the potential to lower the costs of logistics and sensor technology and to improve communication and transparency in complex systems if this is prioritized as a design value. AI has become a critical part of modern warfare. AI equipped military systems can process larger amounts of data more efficiently compared to conventional systems. AI also increases the "self-control, self-regulation, and self-activation of combat systems" due to its inherent computing and decision-making capabilities. Although AI technologies will play a key role in future operational superiority, they are not an end in themselves with regard to the Armed Forces, but rather a means to help them continue in the performance of their missions.

Potential to support operational superiority

In future, military AI applications will be developed that include aspects such as computer vision, intelligent robotics, distributed intelligence, natural language processing, semantic analysis, and data correlation. Strategists and military commanders, in their operational and organizational responsibilities, must be able to take advantage of AI and turn it into a decisive factor of operational superiority. The aim here is to gain speed and room for manoeuvre from better recognition and/or detection of targets and hitherto unknown dangers in the field, from faster and better targeted military action, and from deception actions while ensuring compliance with the laws of war.AI favours a new way of processing data which, combining speed of operation with massive cross- analysis, identifies underlying trends and singularities much more effectively and quickly than a human being could. AI may therefore be expected to bring a fuller and swifter understanding of situations in increasingly complex and interdependent areas of operation.

AI will help to better anticipate the adversary's manoeuvres and optimize operational processes (guidance, gathering, exploitation and dissemination of intelligence). Well-calibrated, it will procure many advantages, for example in the assessment of a threat and optimization of the response to it.

The time saved through AI in accessing and processing data will allow more scope to explore the options under consideration when planning and conducting operations. The AI will make a crucial contribution in relation to weak signals, which can initiate important changes and thus help to scientifically reduce the element of surprise. Feedback data processed by AI will also be integrated into the decision-making process, providing iterative enhancement.

The improved understanding of the situation that AI provides will help to validate options for modes of action and hence step up the pace of decision-making.AI is therefore capable in the short term of ensuring that the armed forces' decision-making processes have the necessary operational superiority to give them the upper hand over many types of adversary.

Optimize flows and resources

Artificial intelligence supports the implementation of predictive models which help to foresee and optimize the logistical flows, technical management of fleets of equipment and scheduling of the associated maintenance, commitments, and recruitment. The use of predictive analytics to optimize flows and resources is a particularly mature AI application which also has a strong dual-use aspect. Consequently, considering the specific features of military operations, AI can quickly bring significant benefits.

Autonomous weapon systems

Automation is increasingly evolving and finding its way through a growing number of industrial and military applications. Engineers have researched for nearly a century and improved vehicle control automation. During World War I, the first autonomous aircraft were produced, and in the 1930s, warships were rebuilt with automation for remote control purposes. Autopilot now can fly an aircraft by itself from take-off to landing. The objective of creating a complete Self-driving vehicle has been in the works for more than two decades. A self-driving vehicle first exhibited autonomous driving on Italian highways in 1998.

Depending on the context, Autonomous weapon systems have already been in existence for more than 70 years. During WWII, guided rockets and cruise missiles were produced. Today's weapons like high precision close air defence system and sophisticated extended range cruise missiles use auto noetic to recognise, locate, select, and lock targets. Although these systems have sophisticated automation, they are usually designed for a particular purpose with limited applications.

The Phalanx is entirely an independent system. It contains special radar for target detection which provides data to an inbuilt computer for calculating target location and guiding the gun for accurate firing. The machine is installed at the location it is meant to defend and is designed to work automatically. When threats come in at a high rate and manual surveillance becomes complicated, the system must be able to run in automatic mode. However, to ensure system safely, there must be and are elaborate protocols to follow while turning the system on to ensure that no accidental damage is caused, and the area must be cleared of friendly vehicles and equipment that may be mistaken for enemy targets. To ensure safe usage of systems, human feedback is exerted by following protocols before the system can be put in automatic mode. Pre-use review, context-dependent use, and strict protocol adherence ensure human supervision and adherence with international humanitarian law.

The **Aegis ballistic missile defence system** offers similar capabilities on a larger scale. In any military confrontation, a commander's discretion to use power must be guided by the basic values of international humanitarian law. **"The behaviour and**

consequences of firearms must be predictable in order to use force discriminatorily and with the requisite care". A commander must be able to anticipate how a missile would respond after it is fired by knowing its impact. As a result, the most significant tactical obstacle posed by increasing firearm autonomy is the need for understanding of the system's actions and responses. Since autonomous systems should be self-contained (autonomous), humans and systems interaction are still required at some level. There is a separate research field that is aimed at studying the relationship between the command structure and how this interface can be constructed. As the behaviour of a machine with many automatic functions can be hard to comprehend, even when operated by humans, the system's control may fail. There have been cases where automatic devices have resulted in fatalities. When introducing more sophisticated automation, designing systems that are intuitive and predictive from the commander's perspective would be a challenge by adopting techniques of machine learning. An even more dilemma with automation is the possibility of antagonistic prevention strategies against any autonomous system. While it is essential for a weaponry system to be coherent for the operator, an opponent may fool a system with predicted actions.

Military applications of machine learning

Machine learning is a term that refers to **"a group of mathematical methods for detecting patterns in data"** and has a broad variety of combat applications. Such methods have been successfully applied to issues in a variety of AI domains. Image identification and speech recognition are two main challenges where those approaches have been successfully used to solve long-standing issues. Machine learning techniques are well suited to heavy data systems where overt device simulation is difficult. Machine learning techniques have been found to be less effective than discrete modelling in applications where the design space is well defined and has a mathematical evaluation (For example, "with equations relating the system's actions and responses to the environment"). In systems where there is no descriptive model but only a large data collection that indirectly determines the characteristics of the system's universe, machine learning methods are suitable for generating a system model. Machine learning is now being used in more and more applications. Some of the broad fields in which machine learning is being used includes: -

Anomaly detection. Pattern detection could possibly be done using "machine learning techniques". The techniques are used to detect data structures that vary from the usual state by detecting patterns of 'normality' in the data (i.e., outliers).

Reconnaissance and surveillance applications. Reconnaissance and monitoring devices today gather massive volumes of data. A UAV with imaging sensors will stay in the air for long periods of time, transmitting data to a data centre for review. The information is then extracted by researchers.

Data processing is one application where machine learning techniques can be beneficial.

Decision-support systems. These systems are utilised in several fields, including medical testing systems, engineering, and marketing, to assist operators in making choices by analysing data and recommending actions. Many weapons research programmes employ machine learning methods for a variety of purposes.

A weapon, or any military system, must undergo extensive assessment, testing, and evaluation before being deployed. Since firearms are meant to cause damage, they are vulnerable to cause accidental harm or injuries when used in an unexpected or unintended manner or circumstance. As a result, being able to comprehend and foresee how a weapon system would act is critical. As a result, weapon system engineers employ restrictive production methods that require rigorous monitoring and verification procedures. Despite the fact that machine learning methods have proved to be useful in variety of fields, they are still under-utilised in weapon systems. The complexity is one rationale in verifying "black box" programmes, which are a characteristic of machine learning-based systems. When integrating machine learning approaches into weapon system development, both technological and organisational problems are likely to emerge. The implied modelling approach complicates research and verification processes, and the structures begin to become complicated. It would be difficult to use machine learning when satisfying military standards for predictability and ability to interpret the system's actions.

Cyber security

Intrusion detection is a vital component of data defence since it prevents malicious network behaviour until it jeopardises information access, integrity, or confidentiality. An intrusion detection system detects intrusions by classifying network traffic as common or disruptive. However, since regular network activity also has a signature that resembles real attacks, cyber security researchers examine the condition with all intrusion warnings to decide whether an actual attack has taken place. Although signature-based IDS may also identify well-known attack patterns, they are unable to detect previously undetectable attacks. Furthermore, since signature-based identification necessitates a high level of skill, it is also slow and costly to create. This makes it difficult for the infrastructure to respond to quickly changing cyber challenges.

Many experiments have used deep learning and other artificial intelligence approaches to enhance the accuracy of detection of documented threats, detect irregular network traffic (which may mean new attack patterns that differ from normal network traffic), and automate model creation.

However, only a few of these systems are used for real information. Lack of training data, wide heterogeneity of network traffic, high cost of errors, and difficulty conducting relevant tests are all difficulties that intrusion detection faces. While vast quantities of network traffic can be obtained, the data is frequently vulnerable and can only be anonymized in portion. Another option is to use virtual results, but this is rarely practical enough. The data must then be labelled for supervised learning to determine whether the patterns are natural or intrusive, as well as for guaranteed anomaly detection, which is always difficult. Finally, the models must be straightforward for researchers to comprehend the recognition limits and importance of features.

Penetration checking during compliance assessments is another way to improve cyber security by identifying easily exploitable security flaws. Owing to the difficulty and vast number of hosts on many networks, penetration testing is often automated. Artificial intelligence (AI) can be used to simulate penetration testing using logical network models rather than the actual network. Graphs or attack trees are commonly used to depict how an adversary can exploit vulnerabilities to gain access to a system. Future penetration research tests will use cognitively valid models of the attacker-defender relationship, as well as deep learning methods to explore the vast problem space of potential attacks.

Missile, air, and space defences
Standard defence systems' aiming abilities may be greatly improved using machine learning techniques. For decades, missile and air defence programmes have focused on automation. During

World War II, the Mark 56gun fire control system was developed. Air defence systems have used artificial intelligence (AI) technologies called "Automated target recognition (ATR)" since the 1970s to detect, find, prioritise, and select incoming air threats quickly and efficiently than a human could. Though, owing to the challenges involved with the production of target libraries, these systems' target-identification capabilities have advanced slowly. Using standard AI programming techniques, the developers of an ATR framework must send a wide and meaningful sample of data on target in all possible variations of its operating environment. This is a difficult challenge in a variety of types and organisational scenarios. Machine learning advances, especially deep learning and generative adversarial networks (GANs) may make this process far easier. Generative modeling is an unsupervised learning task in machine learning that involves automatically discovering and learning the regularities or patterns in input data in such a way that the model can be used to generate or output new examples that plausibly could have been drawn from the original dataset. Engineers may use deep learning techniques to teach ATR systems not only how to differentiate between object groups, but also how to distinguish among military and civilian objects (e.g., a commercial aircraft and a strategic bomber). Engineers may use simulated data to train and test an ATR system in simulation using GANs and produce practical performance. The ATR system skilled using these machine learning methods will outperform an ATR system trained using conventional approaches by a large margin.

Autonomous systems also have new defence techniques in the face of incoming attacks. To supplement conventional air defences, remotely operated vehicles may be used as detonators or flying mines. Advances in swarming and the multi vehicle control may also enable remote operated vehicles to coordinate their activities and carry out advanced air defence manoeuvres. Such systems would increase deterrence against conventional and nuclear attacks by mitigating the threat of manned platforms (e.g., battle planes and armed bombers) and making the outcome of unmanned vehicles (e.g., missiles) more unpredictable.

Electronic warfare

In the same way as machine learning can enhance cyber warfare, it can also improve electronic warfare. Machine learning improves anti-jamming capability on the defensive side by allowing for automated detection and defence against emerging enemy signals. In 2016, the US Defense Department's "Advanced Research Projects Agency (DARPA)" issued an open challenge to develop systems that can identify and analyse new enemy signals as they emerge, rather than after they've been identified, as is the case now. Machine learning can be used on the offensive side to create new jamming techniques that could also be used in a left-of-launch action.

Logistics & Transportation

In military planning and transportation, AI is supposed to play a critical role. Effective military operations include efficient transportation of goods, ammunition, armaments, and soldiers. AI inclusion of military transportation will minimise transportation costs while also reducing human participation. Furthermore, military fleets will easily detect anomalies and anticipate component faults. The United States Army and IBM partnered to use IBM's Watson artificial intelligence tool to anticipate **"maintenance problems in Stryker combat vehicles"**.

Target Recognition

In dynamic battle settings, AI strategies are being developed to enhance target detection accuracy. The use of artificial intelligence in object detection systems increases the systems' ability to locate targets. AI-enabled goal detection systems may include probabilistic predictions of enemy actions, accumulation of weather and environmental variables, anticipation and identification of potential supply line bottlenecks or weak points, analyses of task approaches, and recommended mitigation strategies.

Battlefield Healthcare

To provide remote surgical assistance and rescue operations in war zones, AI can be paired with **"robotic surgical systems (RSS)"** and **"robotic ground platforms (RGP)".** The US is active in the implementation of RSS, RGP, and a variety of other frontline health care programmes. AI-enabled technologies can analyse soldiers' medical records and help in complicated diagnosis in challenging situations.

Combat Simulation & Training

Simulation incorporates systems engineering, software development, and computer science to create computational simulations that familiarise troops with the different combat systems used in military operations. Militaries are actively involved in investment in simulation and training softwares to improve combat efficiency.

Threat Monitoring & Situational Awareness

Intelligence, monitoring, and reconnaissance (ISR) operations are important for threat detection and situational awareness. In support of several military tasks, ISR operations are used to collect and store information. "Unmanned aerial vehicles (UAVs)", also known as drones, with built-in artificial intelligence (AI) can track border zones, detect possible threats, and relay information to response teams.

CHAPTER-5

Impact of AI on character of Warfare

Artificial intelligence (AI) is advancing at a breakneck pace, with far-reaching societal and military implications. Experts who advocate for a low effect are mostly associated with the technological aspects of AI and military organisations' readiness to use it. They argue that the issues that could arise as a result of AI's use would make it unsuitable for military purposes. AI would have an influence on military institutions and battle ideology by encouraging humans to concentrate on what really counts. When applied to ISR activities, AI could free up humans to concentrate on the sample points or photographs that are most likely to be useful, rather than trawling through thousands of political establishment images.

Heavy impacts will be seen in future in areas of military organizations and combat philosophy with increase in AI automation. Autonomous vehicles will persist longer on the battlefield by becoming faster, move secretive, smaller, and more numerous. This improvement is going to make the human involvement on the tactical level minimum, giving them room to focus on much bigger and important strategic issues. An increasingly automated and mechanized system of fighting will also make outcome prediction more accurate and reliable. Hence, fundamental changes in military organizations and combat philosophy are going to cause an overall decrease in the frequency of war. Nations would only fight when they have fully studied the impacts of their attacks and have analysed the gains from such wars.

As in the digital realm, the defence sector does not necessarily open a new path to AI advancement but rather takes advantage of advances in civil uses, adapting them to their benefit. Therefore, the armed forces must find the right balance between benefiting from the things that large digital and often foreign private companies can offer, without becoming dependent on them, while developing their own applications military. The military systems are often embedded and deployed in open unknown environments. So, any AI system designed for Military must meet stringent requirements for latency and robustness. Due to volatile and field deployment of forces, these systems will have access to low power resources and limited speed connections to data centres increasing their complexity even more. They must also be systematically prequalified before being put into service to ensure that they perform as required.

Concerns have been voiced regarding emergence of a "AI arms race" or a "AI cold war that threatens us all", especially amid China and United States. Algorithm-based computer systems are increasingly improving their ability to self-optimize their performance using a number of strategies, many of which are linked to pattern recognition and data matching. This has the potential to boost machine systems' ability to conduct different vital military tasks with a higher degree of autonomy. This has encouraged the strategic thinkers to discuss the ethical and moral ramifications of computer programmes that threaten or strike humans without direct human control at platforms. The main subject of debate at the 1980 Convention on Certain nuclear weapons (CCW) was use of robotic devices in traditional warfare.

CHAPTER 6

AI Meets Nuclear Weapons

When nuclear domain is taken into consideration, the concerns regarding the effects of artificial intelligence on the character of war are amplified. There is a general consensus that launch decisions might not be much improved if artificial intelligence systems take over the control. However, the system of early warnings and notifications can be greatly improved by use of AI. AI systems are considered to act and react in runtime time environment more efficiently, but decreased reaction time increases the likelihood of increased vulnerability of such systems in conflict situations. This could cause accidental or misperceived escalation. Enough amount of training wartime data for AI systems in both conventional battle and nuclear related decisions is a huge concern.. There has to be a way to limit the consequences of actions once the situation seems to be getting out of hand and unexpected damages are caused. A balance should be achieved between desire for a quick response and minimizing unwanted consequences. There are concerns about "hyper war" or "battlefield singularity," where the fast speed of AI-enabled instructions and action completely outpaces the capacity of human decision making, leading to minimum human control over war. An example from Cuban Missile Crisis, shows how the course of action regarding the Soviet Union attacks changed when US leaders changed their minds after analysing the consequences of their actions. If an AI system was pre delegated at that time with set of data it would not have the same ability to mull over its action and reverse course. An effective and reliable AI system requires heaps of real time as well as simulated data for training, verification and validation purposes. Possible Run time decisions taken by commanders close to the launch of weapons can help in assembling data for training purposes of AI enabled systems. The famous Petrov case highlights the importance of human control over AI enabled systems.

During the winters of 1983, the Soviet automated missile warning system gave signals of detection of five incoming US intercontinental ballistic missiles (ICBMs). The officer on duty, reportedly made a quick assessment of the impact of such an attack and the impact of reaction to be taken. He made the judgement that it was an unusually small number of missiles required to initiate nuclear apocalypse and immediately reported malfunctioning of the Soviet system. So, an AI system should be smart enough to differentiate between the actual threat and system malfunction. Since the unpredictability of nuclear weapons continues to be a big concern with no conclusive theory, nuclear safety — including accidents, almost-launches, and missing nuclear warheads—cannot be ensured. History is filled with examples of such miscalculated weapon launches by automated systems. One such example is the case of the US Patriot missiles that shot down friendly planes in 2003. Therefore, launch authorities given to nuclear weapons have the potential to cause catastrophic accidents with worldwide consequences.

Artificial intelligence and nuclear weapons doctrines

Analysts have expressed concerns that adopting advances in AI-related research (e.g., machine learning) and expanding the autonomation of nuclear command and control and early warning systems could increase the risk of nuclear weapons being utilized resulting in a disastrous incident or having a variety of other nuclear security implications.

On the other hand quicker and more precise, progressively automated systems may reduce the possibility of nuclear weapons being used in emergency situations by aiding humans in making more informed decisions. Nuclear-weapons-wielding states do not divulge any detail about their existing or proposed "nuclear early-warning or command-and-control systems". Because of this anonymity, determining the magnitude or existence of the effect that more autonomous computer systems would have in operation is difficult. Nonetheless, based on the limited data available about "nuclear early-warning and command-and-control systems during the Cold War", predictions about how AI could affect them can be made.

Machine devices were usually less technologically advanced during the Cold War period than they are today, and it is impossible to discern any autonomy in their service. Nonetheless, these devices have a telling effect on human nuclear command-and-control decisions, which is important at present and, in future, when AI will allow for more autonomous functionality. According to some researchers, "Services integrating autonomy at rest run virtually, in software, and provide strategy and specialist advisory systems, while systems incorporating autonomy in motion have a physical appearance and include robots and autonomous vehicles". When it comes to nuclear weapons control, this is how resting autonomy can impair human cognitive.

The rationale for automating nuclear command and control

US and the former Soviet Union had the largest

nuclear weapons during Cold War, and each built a sophisticated nuclear force-based infrastructure, as well as command and control systems, to locate and alert of a nuclear attack by the other. The most significant factor in the design of these systems was to ensure nuclear retaliatory capability in the event of an attack. Despite the fact that the geopolitical and technical environment has shifted radically since the end of the Cold War, this imperative remains important in the Russian and US structures almost a decade later. Rather than a relational struggle between the two global powers and their corresponding partners as in cold war, there are more complex potential conflict chains that could involve many nuclear-armed states in various configurations. Furthermore, newer developments like "missile defence, hypersonic rockets, surface-launched anti-satellite (ASAT) systems, and aggressive cyber capabilities" have geopolitical consequences for nuclear security that are still unknown. Nonetheless, United States and the Soviet Union focused their energy, technologies, and other resources on ensuring that each could launch on alert of a nuclear attack by the other.

Beginning in the 1950s, both nations established nuclear capabilities, which included manned bombers, intercontinental ballistic missiles (ICBMs), and air launched nuclear missiles. This involved careful preparation, order, and control. For reference, beginning in 1960, the United States implemented a Single Coordinated Operating Strategy (SIOP), which included precautionary and retaliatory tactics for massive nuclear attacks on locations in the China and Soviet alliance. These necessitated a number of automated systems and comprehensive planning, including in-flight refuelling for bombers and the Strategic Automated Command and Control System (SACCS), which assures reliable transfer of launching orders.

To incorporate data from different sources in decision making systems, they each built extensive and hardened communications, control, and response systems. With the extreme time pressures involved in determining when a nuclear attack is taking place, they had to use technology to guarantee that intelligence regarding attack met human decision makers. During the Cold War, both sides were worried with the possibility of enemy nuclear bombers. Each country developed a sensor network to detect such threats. United States developed the Distant Early Warning Line (DEW) in 1950s. During this time, they also tested a computer-controlled air defence system called "Semi-Automatic Ground Environment (SAGE)" to destroy Soviet bombers flying over US airspace. The USSR, on the other hand, quickly followed ICBMs, prompting the US to abandon SAGE. These missiles adopt ballistic trajectories that send them mostly outside of the atmosphere, making them impossible to intercept. Furthermore, both sides' construction of nuclear-powered ballistic missile submarines (SSBNs) boosted the possibility of nuclear missiles originating closer to targets and emerging from unknown locations, resulting in less time to react. As a result, more to augment early warning systems more modern radar systems and satellites were developed.

Automation and the Dead Hand

US and Soviet Union had nearly identical "nuclear early-warning and command-and-control structures". Late in the Cold War, USSR failed to match the US satellite-based launch-detection system. Soviet technology seemed to fall behind than US. The Soviet ground detection network had a small range of coverage as well. After the Soviet invasion of Afghanistan in 1979, the US raised its armed forces in the first half of the 1980s. President Ronald Reagan called the Soviet Union an "evil tyranny" and proposed an anti-missile system to protect the US from nuclear strike. If such missile defences were put in place, the Soviet Union feared that a US first nuclear strike would castrate Soviet nuclear command and control, eliminating half of the Soviet Union's nuclear forces before they could be deployed, with US missile defences sweeping up the rest. The "Mertvaya Ruka (Dead Hand)" scheme was brought online by USSR in 1985 and was established in response to Soviet policymakers' concerns regarding ensuring their nuclear retaliatory capability. The workings of Dead Hand have been defined in a variety of ways. It is also confused with Perimeter System, an autonomous signal system that sends radio signals to launch nuclear missiles when all other modes of communication are unavailable. Perimeter may have been used with the dead hand method, but the two are not identical. According to some sources, Dead Hand was a part of the Soviet command-and-control system built to ensure nuclear deterrence in the event of an attack, and it is still operating in Russia today.

The system allowed the Soviet Command to issue nuclear strike orders as a provisional command with defined parameters. After the defined parameters were met, the system would then automatically issue the start command. The system would get data from a number of sensor systems like Nuclear explosion sensors, seismic systems, radiation detection systems, and wind pressure evidence. The Dead Hand device also seemed to be capable of operating in a semi-automated manner, requiring no command authority to initiate an attack. The machine would have to ensure that all conditions were met before issuing such a launch order. The preliminary command was created first. The machine would then determine whether the USSR had been targeted by a nuclear bomb. If that proved to be the case, the machine would search to see if the communication system with the Soviet command authority is available. If communication systems are down, the machine would assume that possible nuclear attack has taken place. It could delegate launch authority to whoever was in charge of the device at the time, obviating the need for many levels of traditional command authority.

Future of AI in nuclear early warning and command and control

For advanced warning and target detection, automation is becoming increasingly important. Dead Hand was neither a self-contained nor a "intelligent" weapon. It was almost of an automatic telephone exchange, since it was regulated by clear if–then conditions. Automation has progressed a lot since the 1980s, thanks in part to the availability of much more computing resources. Machines still struggle with conceptual thought, despite these and other advancements allowing them to achieve greater autonomy in some situations. This is still a tricky problem for AI researchers to solve. Even though recent media attention has focused on the antiquated existence of some elements of the Soviet and US nuclear force command systems, automation has a wide and growing impact on sensing, tracking, analysis, and many other nuclear command and control functions. (For example, it was discovered in 2016 that "**SACCS**, which had been extinct since 1963, was still working on floppy discs, a 1970s technology".) Machine learning tools would be surprising if they weren't already being used to solve specific nuclear threats like identification and early warning, as well as target recognition.

Project Maven, which integrates AI—specifically, deep neural networks—into the battle against the Islamic State group, is an example of how the US Department of Defence uses such techniques to triage and analyse data sets.

Experts say the problem of mediation AI use is urgent, citing rapid technological advancement in AI and its many potential collisions with nuclear policy.

CHAPTER-7

International Landscape

Stephen Hawking, a late British scientist, once said, "Governments seem to be engaged in an AI arms race, designing planes and weapons with intelligent technologies."

Many countries have recently released civilian artificial intelligence strategies. This acceleration and the global emulation that goes with it bear witness to the shared impression that AI expertise is an essential power factor for the future. The various AI strategies published recently reveal a global hierarchy of AI power.

The two superpowers, the USA and China are beyond the reach of other nations, each of which controls a vast mass of data and has an ecosystem based on powerful, global integrators (GAFA and BATX) and is in a position to use its scientific and financial resources to further increase its domination.

An emerging intermediate power, the EU, whose tough approach to legal and ethical issues can be a strength or a weakness depending on its impact (standardization power, underpinned by many actors in the public and private sectors, versus the risk of research or entrepreneurship development policy that is hindered by excessive regulation).

The second circle of countries, including France, Germany, the UK, Japan, South Korea, Singapore, Israel, and Canada, which have certain advantages but not sufficient critical mass. The extent of their autonomy will depend on the leverage they can extract from the cooperation's they are able to establish and the relevance of niche strategies that maximize their comparative advantages.

Canada, Japan, Singapore, China, the United Arab Emirates, Finland, Denmark, France, the United Kingdom, the European Commission, South Korea, India, and others all launched AI application and growth strategies in 2017 and 2018. They are focused on scientific research, talent development, skills and education, public and private sector adoption, ethics and inclusion, standards and regulations, and data and digital infrastructure. Therefore, it seems that nations will compete in AI science, investment, and expertise.

There is a fundamental difference between the two major players, the United States and China. The latter can guide private-sector actors with a firmer hand and instruct them to cooperate with the public sphere, including the military. China has thus come up with the doctrine of "civil-military fusion" designed to maximize transfers between research, industry, the state and the armed forces. In the Chinese model, AI applications are firmly extended to the security sphere. Relations are more complicated in the United States, where the reluctance of certain companies to work with the Department of Defence has already disrupted certain projects, such as Maven. These social and institutional aspects are the main distinction between US-China.

The race to secure the resources needed to develop AI has already begun and is expected to intensify. The resources in question are both intangible (capturing scarce human resources) and tangible (capturing key technologies, etc.). Technological development has been accompanied among all actors by an awareness of the ethical implications of AI. International debates, on the other hand, have tended to focus on the potential production of lethal autonomous weapons systems (LAWS). A Group of Government Experts (GGE) on the subject was set up under the Convention on Certain Conventional Weapons (CCCW) in 2017 to study the ethical implications of use of AI in Military.

AI In USA Army

In comparison to the relatively stable political systems in authoritarian states like China or Russia, the US-American landscape of governmental policy proposing the use of Artificial Intelligence within its military security apparatus is much more fragmented, de-centralized, and lacks stringency.

Conventional US war has seen with the 2001 and 2003 invasions of Afghanistan and Iraq, a strategic re-orientation of its operations towards semi-autonomous (armed) drones and vehicles within its arsenal, in addition to officially including cyberspace within the range of battlefields in which the US Army is active.

The Obama administration institutionalized these changes in 2009 by founding a central authority of the US Army's operations in cyberspace on par with its other conventional legs on land, in the air, at sea, and in space, the US Cyber Command, representing the currently most active military unit engaged in defending the US from external cyberattacks and disrupting the communications and tactics of the campaigns of its enemies today.

In 2016, the Department of Defence pushed the topic of "autonomy" in military on its research and development institutions, first under the newly elevated Office of the Secretary of Defence. The Defence Science Board proposed 25 policy recommendations to strengthen trust in autonomous systems back in 2016. The plan encouraged both the executive branch as well as the ground personnel within the US defence apparatus to entangle the private high-technology sector more closely with the armed forces by incubating defence-oriented private projects through federal expenditure, and to generally accelerate and intensify domestic investment in AI to "help the United States maintain military advantage through increasing use of autonomy." Later that year the White House issued its first "National Artificial Intelligence Research and Development Strategic Plan" to streamline its efforts to modernize and accelerate the federal capabilities using AI as well as to boost the national economy developing AI applications and expanding its use to all public sectors, including civil and strategic.

In 2014, the Washington-based progressive **Centre for New American Security (CNAS)**, the think-tank closest to the Obama White House concerned with security policy, proposed an overarching security strategy handling the "daily tactical game of foreign policy manoeuvring" and assessing contest over military-technical superiority, and whether the United States can sustain its advantage deep into the 21st century or be over- taken by its competitors," called the "Third off set." The name references two previous technology-cantered national security strategies, namely when the Eisenhower administration stressed the necessity of maximizing nuclear deterrence against the quantitative superiority of the Warsaw Pact armies in the 1950s, and when the administrations of the 1970s and 1980s updated the precision and variability of conventional weapons in reaction to the rise of asymmetrical warfare

All of these "off sets," exemplify the undertaken paradigms shifts from "unguided weapons regime" to a "guided weapons regime" during the first half of the twentieth century, emphasizing the act that the technological advances in space-assisted navigation, communication and sensory-guided weapons engineered the upheaval of Soviet superiority over Eurasia based on their over-whelming numbers. Thus "offsetting" the otherwise impermeable security risk. Former US Secretary of Defence Chuck Hagel summarized in 2014, "all this suggests that [the United States] are coming to an era in which American supremacy in the oceans, skies and space, without referring to cyberspace, erstwhile cannot be hypothesized, "and laid the foundation for his successor Ashton B. Himsel holding a PhD in theoretical physics from Oxford University and a regular guest lecturer at Stanford, Carter to establish a new alliance between the corporate innovation hubs in Silicon Valley and the Defence Department through the Defence Innovation Unit Experimental institution (DIUx), an interface to network and crossover talent and ideas between the private and public sectors to the benefit of both.

The US-American information and communications sectors are leading the drive to innovate autonomous solutions. These industries invest over ten times more money in research and development than the US-American private and public aerospace and defence sector combined.

Surprisingly, the strategy to better integrate the private sector into the strategic planning of the Pentagon has not been so effective due to growing public mistrust following the NSA surveillance scandal or the inauguration of President Trump and his administrations' variant fixation on near-term goals.

On a visit to DIUx and Silicon Valley in 2017, President Trump's Secretary of defence approved investing more than $100 million in 45 contracts that explored ideas to get the human element out of hot battlefields to put the American soldiers in operating positions away from danger. In the middle of 2017, the Defence Department established **Project Maven**, an effort to seamlessly integrate commercial image-recognition software into the analytical capacities of UAVs to take out the labour-intensive human analysis of their video feeds. Recently it surfaced that the Pentagon is using a variant of Google's open-source Tenor Flow AI system under a private-public partnership. Thus, it can be said that the Trump administration followed the groundwork laid out by its predecessor to invest into strategic applications of AI technology, however, a cautionary Department of Defence is staying clear of developing such technology themselves and have only limited capability to engage the private sector to participate in their interest in offsetting China's advances in emerging weapons technologies.

AI In Chinese Army

In contrast to US-American pluralism fragmented between industrial and political interest groups, China's increasing centralization of its one-party government has recognized and internalized the joint potential of emerging technologies under President Xi more than any other nation-state. Nominally, the United States are holding an advantage in the numbers of high-tech start-ups and global corporations developing AI, an environment also nourished by attracting the most eager and intelligent Chinese students to seek education at American campuses and thus feeding the need or talent in Silicon Valley and across the US to fill the telecommunications companies' well-paid and highly competitive positions. Beijing's long-term goals to emerge as a global economic and strategic power has catalysed heavy domestic and foreign investments in emerging technologies.

These include rapidly upgrading the naval and air forces to gradually expand China's anti-entry / denial-of-territory zone away from coastal borders, diversifying the domestically manufactured and designed civil and military satellite systems, and pioneering high-end telecommunications in space, as well as promoting Chinese Telecommunications companies with affordable budget plans and top-to-bottom changes in government policy to meet the needs of their research and development departments. The growing volume of Chinese foreign investment in US-American high-tech start-ups and publicly-held telecom corporations led the Trump administration to tighten regulatory oversight to shield US-American intellectual property: "The Chinese have found a way around our protections, our safeguards, on technology transfer in foreign investment. And they are using it to pull ahead of us, both economically and militarily," James Lewis from the Centre of Security and International Studies argues.

China's is using its huge capital to gain influence within foreign AI developers while cradling and catalysing its own AI industry within China's domestic economy accumulated in "The Internet Plus and Artificial Intelligence Plan (2016-18)," the world's most broadly state-supported policy plan calling or breakthroughs in AI development and its expansive applications, including in unmanned systems and cyber-security, clearly exemplifying the importance of AI technology in the eyes of the Chinese government.

As part of the 13th Five-Year-Plan for the years 2016-2020, the Chinese governments' Artificial Intelligence Plan represented a stepping- stone between prioritizing its development on ministerial level as the sixth most important task for the country and enshrining it as part of China's self-identity. The 2017's government work report, the Chinese Premier's annual report to the Congress on the past years' economic performance and the coming years' challenges featured Artificial Intelligence for the first time, stressing the need to divest funds into its adoption, followed by President Xi enshrining AI development as a key driver to China's hegemonic ambitions to become a "science and technology superpower" which he also highlighted in his opening speech to the 19th Party Congress in November 2017.

Precisely, the plan sets the national goal of expanding its AI industry to $23.8 billion gross output by 2020, a tenfold increase from 2016, in an overall plan to be the world's leader in AI development by 2025. By 2030, the plan envisions, the target gross output to be set at $150 billion in core AI industries innovating and developing the software architecture and hardware infrastructure and $1.5 billion in adjacent AI-enhanced industries developing applications of automation in all sectors, e.g., self driving vehicles. In context to various analyses of the global AI market these targets all are within the high end of market forecasts.

In accordance with the monumental effort to modernize the PLA's capabilities, by researching, developing, and producing nuclear-powered submarines, operational aircraft and helicopter carriers, as well as China's first domestically produced passenger and cargo jet on top of its already successful modern generation of fighter jets, its leadership has closely studied the US Army's concentration on autonomy and the Defence Department's proposed "Third Off set" strategy. In fact, China's efforts in researching and developing its own swarming-capable or solitary UAVs, semi-autonomous missile guiding systems, and the growing frequency and scope of the PLA's practical mission experience borrow heavily from the strategic idea of asymmetrically off setting an otherwise quantitatively too powerful competitor through technological superiority.

The government's work report cites Lieutenant General Liu Ghuozhi, Director of the Central Military Commission's Science and Technology Commission, saying that **"whichever nation is not prepared to engage in developing Artificial Intelligence appli-**

cations for its military will be disrupted!"

Following this imperative, Chinese scientists and military officials call for a "military-civil union" of both corporate and government research facilities and programs to ensure the maximum mutual benefit, ultimately arguing for such a fusion to progress national defence. Parallel to prioritizing AI development since 2016, the Chinese government has established the "Military-Civil Fusion Development Commission" under direct leadership of President Xi, while high-ranking PLA generals already occupy leading roles in both military and civil research departments.

AI in Russian Army

The Soviet Union has always been reluctant to play a vital part for control autonomy of nuclear weapons and associated systems. In the fields of nuclear ballistic missile defence, command and control, early warning including strike abilities, the autonomy was pervasive but human involvement can never be substituted. The USSR conducted its first nuclear test on August 29, 1949, making it the second nuclear-armed country in the world after the United States. In 1950s, this fuelled research in computer science as well as in the field of autonomy.

Autonomy in missile defence and early warning

The nuclear forces requirements of the USSR drove the advancement of computer science to a large extent. In early 1960s, Ballistic missile defence (BMD) and early warning systems sparked advancements in computer science. In the 1950s, it was visible that computers could play an important role in detecting and intercepting incoming warheads. Automation and autonomy were the basic requirements in their design to make the majority of BMD and early-warning systems. With the necessity of speed and early-warning for BMD, it is difficult for a human being to strive with machines data processing. As per estimation, the USSR's collective budget for system research and expansion on BMD including advance warning from 1950-1970 exceeded the total budget for the Soviet missile and space programmes. The main expenditure was on the computer development. Nevertheless, ratification of 1972 on US and Soviet Anti-Ballistic Missile Treaty (ABM) permitted USSR to shift their primacies and expend superfluous on advance warning system, belligerent nuclear weapons and command & control system.

Autonomy in early warning systems

There have always been concerns in the USSR about the nuclear arsenal's survivability. As a result, before the end of Cold War, the Soviet nuclear posture was based on the principle of **"start on warning."** The Soviet leadership was prepared for a nuclear strike against the United States as soon as early warning systems detected a launch. The start on warning enhanced the role of early warning system. In 1972, USSR designed an integrated, multi-layered early warning system. The Soviet Union built a network of radars and warning satellites based on this idea. The integrated early warning system is intended to automatically collect data from a variety of sources. In a practical combat situation, operators might have an inadequate time to examine data collected automatically from the early warning system. But the system was not able to achieve its full capacity, which was predicted in 1972. The Soviet commanders did not believe the capacity achieved was completely credible. Several times, the early-warning system misidentified incoming missiles. In 1983, an occurrence with the **Oko (Eye) early-warning system** is the most well-known examples of a false alarm. This system had two satellites i.e Oko-1 and Oko-2, that were able to track missile's hot plume to determine its trajectory. The early warning system detected missile attacks. Lieutenant Colonel Stanislav Petrov, commander of Oko command centre, had no way to cross check the data. He was to interpret the data on the display and inform his superiors. He had no say in whether or not to respond with a nuclear strike. The Oko system was source of information for a possible attack on the Soviet Union. It was revealed afterwards that no other sources were used to support the Oko alert of 1983.

On other hand, the danger of an erroneous humanoid command built on a wrong alarm was alarming. The early warning system continued to deteriorate after the fall of the Soviet Union. As a result, the Russian military's role in nuclear command and control has been reduced. Russian nuclear plans no longer included the principle of launch-on-warning.

Automation of command and control

ABM Treaty was enforced in 1972. According to treaty both USA and USSR could employ BMD system to protect only one area. The Soviet Union made the decision to defend Moscow. The only possibility for USSR to avoid US first strike in the absence of BMD was to make second strike capability to evade first strike. US and the Soviet Union both acquired second nuclear strike capability in order to prevent launching a first nuclear strike against each other. In the 1990 Joint Statement on Future Nuclear and Space Arms Negotiations, the principle was quoted as a key principle of "enhancing strategic stability."

Two years after the ABM Treaty, the Soviet government begin research programs on a highly automated Perimeter command and control system in 1974. The objective of this system was to launch counter-attack with all accessible means if enemy launched a first strike on Soviet territory and the political and military leadership were unable to function normally, whether due to communications disruption or amputation of the leadership.

There were two ways to warn the perimeter. It can be notified by a human in the first case. Perimeter could also alert itself basing on data from earth surface, sea, air, and space-based sensors if it receives data confirming a nuclear outbreak. The system then asks the General Staff of the Armed Forces to respond with a yes or no. If the commander-in-chief (nowadays Russia's president) subsists the first strike and is also within range, General Staff will give its decision to the Perimeter system. If Perimeter does not obtain a response from the General Staff, it must rely on the ostensible nuclear briefcase 'Cheget', part of Strategic Rocket Forces' 'Kazbek' command-and-control system, for a yes or no response. If the nuclear briefcase does not respond, Perimeter asks for a response from any Strategic Rocket Forces command centre. Perimeter is only intended to launch retaliation after obtaining no response from any other sources. As it is pre-requisite for Perimeter to get alert after receiving information from detectors that confirms a nuclear strike has transpired, it's difficult to envision that it may get activated without any nuclear attack or when attacker had only used conventional and cyber resources. In unlikely event if Perimeter gets activated without any nuclear attack, the system status is made such that it will become visible to all authorised military and political leadership and all decisions taken by system can be reversed at any time by them. Perimeter is still built on the concept of keeping a human in the loop while still permitting for wholly automated operation.. Colonel Valery Yarynich, a former officer of the Strategic Rocket Forces and later the General Staff In an interview in 2009 outlined the Perimeter system's full operational capacity and indicated that it was "constantly being upgraded." During its operational employment. The Perimeter system was decommissioned in 1995 as part of the nuclear weapons decommissioning process when it no longer served a purpose at the termination of Cold War.

Russia took this decision on its own, without the United States taking similar deactivating measures. The system was not destroyed, but it was rendered non-operational. However, some of the infrastructure became obsolete over time.

Offensive Posture – The new trend

The prospect of a pre-emptive nuclear strike fortifies an offensive nuclear stance. This strike is designed to prevent an opponent from launching a nuclear or conventional attack. As a result, the highly automated Perimeter system would play a minor role in an offensive nuclear posture. Such a stance would necessitate sensibly calibrated nuclear weapons use. Due to Russia's extremely volatile security climate, the system has been designed in a manner that when the political - strategic leadership are unable to function normally, the defensive nuclear posture retains sufficient automatic command and control to substitute a human-based system. At outset of an armed conflict, this level of command-and-control automation would not be required. However, if skirmish continues with the opponent retaliating, the system may be required to take over.

The usage of Perimeter-style command and control systems in the concluding stages of an armed battle that began with a nuclear defalcation appears to be politically and militarily ineffective. On the other hand, an aggressive nuclear stance might result in a demand for latest nuclear weapons-related abilities. The Poseidon nuclear-powered unmanned underwater vehicle, for example, was unveiled by President Putin in 2018. (UUV). Poseidon (also known as Status-6) is a self-contained system that will run in accordance with commands from command centres when and if it is commissioned. A nuclear energised submarine would launch Poseidon. Based on the payload, which could be a nuclear warhead or monitoring equipment it could carry out a variety of missions. The Poseidon began its underwater trials in late 2018. Before the end of the 2018–27 State Armament Program, the system is planned to be functioning.

AI in Indian Army

With 0.34 million software professionals employed in India, the country is rapidly establishing itself as Asia's software development capital. As per latest, total exports of IT-related goods reached US $9 billion, which is not astounding for a country that produces more than 100,000 IT professionals every year, proving Bill Gates' claim that India is the software superpower. India is now regarded as having exceptional high-performance computing capabilities. Conversely, military has taken longer to adapt to technology and is currently trying to rebalance. The Indian Army published a document called "IT Roadmap 2000" in 1999 that outlined how information technology would be implemented in the military. With such a significant technological and cybernetics advantage, it is reasonable to assume that if India attempted to wage a cyber war against an adversary, the threat would be very powerful and could cause significant harm. Supremacy of India in computer software and hardware manufacture and availability for expert all over the world i.e., US/Western countries and Middle East, provide her a great strategic advantage in AI domain. The Centre for Artificial Intelligence and Robotics by Defence Research and Development Organization (DRDO) has a Centre for Artificial Intelligence and Robotics that is devoted to AI research (CAIR). The institution has nearly 150 competent scientists' and emphases on: -

1.AI Robotics and Control Systems.

2.Command, Control, Communication, and Intelligence Systems.

3.Communication and Networking.

4.Communication Secrecy.

The Laboratory has been concentrating on AI and Communications. It's worth noting that CAIR has already designed robots for non-destructive testing of light combat aircraft composite components (Tejas). The following projects are in development: -

Artificial Intelligence (AI) tools for Net Centric Operations (AINCO), a collection of systems aimed at building a knowledge based receiving and processing semantic data, intrusion reasoning, and event connexion.

Robot family for surveillance and reconnaissance applications (Robeson), a portable robot system designed for reconnaissance, patrolling and surveillance. With an obstacle avoidance function and constant video feedback, it can navigate autonomously in semi-structured environments. The subsequent is a miniature unmanned ground vehicle (UGV) design for low intensity conflict and surveillance in closed environments.

In the Armed Forces, unmanned aerial vehicles (UAVs) are now in use, and unmanned ground vehicles (UGVs) and unmanned water vehicles are on the way. On the battlefield, the robot can play a variety of roles, from sentry to surgeon. This AI force performs hard operations such as mining, demining of launching attack bridges flying over water hazards and para-drop robots in conjunction with special forces. Aside from that, logistics will be entirely operated by robots.

The Indian Armed Forces are currently collaborating closely with CAIR on a project involving the Multi Agent Robotics Framework (MARF). The Snake, a legged robot, UGV and Wall Climber are examples of such robots. Moreover, focus is on the following as well: -

Image interpretation to identify and classify targets an to use AI algorithms to automate the mining of low-level map components from imagery.

Systems for diagnosing and maintaining advanced weapon systems.

Systems for missile target range and trajectory analysis being made for calculating killing zones, launch time and mock-up to help qualify missile efficacy in different scenarios.

Systems for increasing the utilization of robotics in anti-improvised explosive device (IED) extraction, rifle shooting, and other applications.

CHAPTER 8

ARTIFICIAL INTELLIGENCE – POTENTIAL RISKS

Artificial intelligence's introduction into national militaries carries significant risks. Introduction of **lethal autonomous weapons systems (LAWS)** attract a lot of public attention. These systems are prone to raise safety, lawful, philosophical, and principled questions as they make decisions.

AI facilitates the creation of complex systems that are hard to understand, posing issues of accountability and determination if the system is responding as anticipated or planned.

This issue can be alleviated if transparency is given enough weight in AI design. Where it isn't, it's more likely that AI system errors will go unnoticed, whether they're unintentional or triggered by a third party using procedures like bugging or data infecting. As AI will be intrinsic in all systems, the threats related with its use could affect all realms of interest, from intelligence, command and conflict to maintenance, support, and the condition of personnel (state of mind, morale, etc.). AI technologies are not yet mature enough to upset power relations or change the spirit of warfare. It is a fast-moving field, and the steadily declining cost of the technology suggests that new modes of action and uses will emerge in near future. Being easily accessible, especially because of the diversion of commercial technologies or the use of low-cost robots, the accompanying new dangers will soon become much more pressing. Moreover, the increasing use of AI in Military will raise various fears. The fears they raise include:

The possibility that adversative AI will be able to predict our modes of action, depriving us of the element of surprise.

The immobility of our command capabilities because of the neutralization, deception, or distraction of our technologies.

The extension of influence operations and actions targeting the flow of information (disinformation, undermining media credibility, fake news, etc.).

AI Manipulation

The roll-out of artificial intelligence is still in its infancy and often limited to the more error-tolerant use cases. Industrial-scale AI, especially for military use, implies more stringent robustness requirements. The technology is making rapid progress but there are risks inherent in certain techniques. Human perception can be dodged using deep neural networks, for instance by incorporating discrepancies into two images that are imperceptible to the human eye. Learning techniques likewise pose various risks. The adversary can amend learning data or the model to produce an abnormal result, possibly on request. Generally, the quality of learning data is a decisive factor for obtaining robust algorithms. If learning data are non-existent, inaccessible, insufficient, or unsuited to the intended use, the results obtained will not be satisfactory.

Greater Autonomy- Greater risks

Autonomy refers to a robotic system's ability to perform operations quicker than a human or a man-controlled machine might, which is especially appealing to the military for time-dependant operations or tasks like air-to-air warfare, air-defence, or counter measures to cyber-attacks. From a command and control standpoint, autonomy would make robotic systems much more agile, reducing the need for a continuous communication connection between military commanders & these intelligent machines. It may also let military to decrease the manpower and analysts employed to monitor and process data. Autonomy is beneficial for dangerous, dull and dirty missions also because it eliminates constraints (such as complacency, tiredness, boredom, starvation, or distress) that affects efficiency of manpower to deteriorate with time. Autonomy extends the reach of systems. It allows remote-controlled systems access to operational theatres that were previously unavailable or too dangerous for manned operations. Deep water, the Arctic, and, possibly, outer space are examples of zones protected by area-denial/anti-access (AD/A2) schemes and installations with complex & communication restricted working spaces for humans. Finally, autonomy opens up new possibilities for collaborative missions, since weapon systems can be used in huge groups, or "swarms," in a more organised, developed, and strategic way than if they were controlled by a human driver.

Enhancement in autonomy is raising expectations in civil & military setups, as they increase the utility and dependability on robotics, which could result in substantial monetary and operative advantages. Companies, government agencies, and military, may all benefit from a greater reliance on robotic systems to increase manpower efficacy. They may also be able to overcome other operational difficulties linked with crewed actions or the use of technological systems with enhancement in autonomy.

Nonetheless, advances in autonomy have spawned a slew of ethical, regulatory, and security concerns relating to military and civilian applications. The growth of autonomy in systems critical to safety such as weapons or vehicles questions of limitations to be imposed on autonomous systems without direct human control and oversight. The continuing in-house governmental conversation under Certain Conventional Weapons (CCW Convention) & 1980 convention on lethal autonomous weapon systems (LAWS) as well as the debate over semi-autonomous car crashes, have depicted that no easy response to that question exists.

The problem of maintaining a balance between human operability & autonomy has far-reaching and complicated legal repercussions, especially in terms of determining who bears criminal responsibility when an auto-pilot vehicle or autonomous weaponry inflicts harm. According to some legislators, the spread of autonomous vehicles is occurring in an unlawful space or grey area, & it is anticipated to make legal proceedings more complex in case of any fatal incident. Autonomy advancements also invoke fresh security issues. A malicious actor could easily exploit the limits of current systems in terms of decision-making & perceptual intelligence, dodging a system merely by deceiving the sensors or monitoring units. The growing use of and dependence on intelligent systems would inevitably result in significant social changes. It will alter the way businesses, government agencies, and the military run, among other things. UAVs in Air forces, for instance are substituting crewed combat aircrafts with amazingly intelligent remote aerial systems that necessitates shift in selection of staff, training, and operation, with a distant operator taking over control from the pilot, and an establishment supervisor, who resultantly imposes amendments in professional culture.

Before designing and deployment of an artificially intelligent military technology, it's crucial to be aware of the problems that remain unsolved.

In spite of better response, many applications

need improved openness, secure operability, user confidence, and comprehension. Critical security systems, automated agents, spy techniques, health-related and certain applications with comparable standards are all common. With AI's recent advancements, there's been a surge of attention towards transparency studies to help consumers in this regard.

Vulnerabilities

It has been discovered that adjusting the input signal to make the classification system entirely fail is relatively simple. Getting pre-trained models to achieve efficiency is a common practice when constructing a DNN (Deep Neural Network) with just a small amount of training data. Transfer learning is the name given to this notion. Using a model that is acclimatized with large data-sets, replacing and adapting the network's final layers to the particular problem, and then optimising the parameters in the final stages (and sometimes the entire system) using the available training data is a common practise. A considerable number of pre-trained models are now available for download on the internet. The question then becomes, "How do we know that those who uploaded the model have no bad intentions?".

Limitations of AI in Military Applications

ML models aren't transparent or interpretable enough. Using DL to model the control of an autonomous vehicle using a deep neural network (DNN), for example, necessitates hundreds of thousands of parameters. Clearly, such a complicated programme will be difficult to enforce. Even when applied to toy problems, models created using alternative ML algorithms where the model can be presented graphically, such as parse trees or decision trees, are difficult, if not impossible, to understand. The ability, or in this case, inability, of the artificial intelligence system to explain its rationale to the decision maker or human operator is perhaps the most crucial challenge.

Models created with machine learning are known to be vulnerable to attack. Even if the attacker is unaware of the model, a DL-based model can be readily fooled by changing the input signal. A carefully constructed camouflage pattern on the ground, for example, can theoretically fool unmanned aerial vehicles (UAVs) using object detection.

The most important component of any machine learning application is data from which machines can learn and eventually provide information. Military agencies are also adept at gathering information for debriefing or reconstruction. However, there's no guarantee that the same information will be available. For ML, it has been successfully used. As a result, military agencies may need to change their data collection procedures in order to fully utilise modern AI methods like DL.

The limits of automation in Nuclear Doctrine

Both USSR and United States understood the importance of restricted automation in nuclear command and control, and were hesitant to envoy higher-order decision-making functions to automated machines other than special scenarios like missile defence until 1980s. They made attempts to enhance redundancy in systems in case components were damaged, lost, or fail in some way. However, the added complexity of such intelligent systems as a consequence of redundant attributes may be a major cause of failure. Actually, both sides early warning systems had defects and their automatic capabilities were too limited to be entirely trustworthy. Humans "in the loop" in nuclear command and control systems played a critical role in addressing these problems as they emerged. This is shown in the examples below.

In November 1979, data on an incoming nuclear attack was fed into the early-warning system by an accidentally loaded war exercise tape onto a computer at the North American Aerospace Defence Command (NORAD). The capability of NORAD to independently check its radar system was the only way for operators to know the alarm was false. This was the result of a US strategy known as "dual phenomenology," which entails having several, autonomous types of tactical sensors to compare. President Jimmy Carter had the limited time to decide whether or not to retaliate with nuclear retaliation. After few minutes, it was informed that attack was a hoax. The failure of a computer chip worth less than approximately 1.3 US Dollars was ultimately found as the cause of the incident by technicians at the

NORAD command centre.

The Soviet early-warning system, however, did not always have this redundancy because it was costly. Five ICBMs were reported inbound from the US in 1983, according to the Soviet early warning system. The message had to be deciphered by the duty watch officer, Lieutenant Colonel Stanislav Petrov. Petrov rightly considered that if the US knew the Soviet nuclear response would be enormous, why would it assault with only five ICBMs? It was revealed that the system had been deceived by cloud reflections. Although human judgement and contextual thought are imperfect, they were the key in determining the threat in this case.

Impact on human decision-making

Algorithm-based systems operate at a very high rate (milliseconds) to process data and perform functions. Studies reveal that these algorithm-based machines can work at super speed only after they have deep learned the patterns on which decisions are made. Google in recent past started a project namely **"Maven"** primarily to digitize data for image recognition of real-time footage from a drone. It was one of the early attempts to manifest how AI could apply in decision-making for state's defence forces by replacing human operators in data processing units. Purpose of this project was to enable soldiers to process data of insurgent's weapons and tools two to three times faster. It's difficult to add proprietary limitations to Project Maven's software since it's based on the open-source Tensor Flow library.

Many people are concerned about the increasing impact of automation in military decision-making, particularly in terms of nuclear deterrence. The present condition of automated systems is analogous to a black box, in which retracing the function of making decision is not achievable. The inability of track and trace in decision-making is a serious issue since the operator must trust the device's outcome. The AI programs utilize the data provided to them to learn their operations. As a result, if it misrepresents the situation's reality, it's impossible to rule out the possibility of unintentional escalation. When combined with existing advances in missile technology and hypersonic weapons, AI could create an ecosystem that could drastically decrease the time it takes to respond to a nuclear attack.

Unpredictability and vulnerabilities of AI technology

Due to the black box characteristics of algorithm based systems, the military faces a huge accountability challenge as AI research programmes continue. Consistency is a hallmark of conventional military organisation behaviour. If machine learning algorithms are used in destructive autonomous weapon systems (LAWS), the accountability issue will become much worse, and it will become even worse if machine learning algorithms are ever incorporated in nuclear bombs. Failures in systems and their effects are unimaginable in these circumstances. The 2016 DARPA Cyber Grand Challenge, first ever hacking challenge in which autonomous "capture the flag" systems competed, gave an early example of such a scenario, though not in the nuclear domain. One independent system failed in the middle of the contest, while one other paralyzed the system that it was to protect. The likelihood of nuclear attack caused by the failure of nuclear warheads controllers initiated by a computational system is remote, as it meant that verdict to set off a nuclear firearm would be done automatically. States, on the other hand, still want to retain that decision with the man in charge. Unplanned escalation triggered by misleading data provided by a machine learning algorithm, on the other hand, seems to be a more likely scenario that must be addressed if nuclear weapons are ever equipped with machine learning algorithms. If adversaries were able to provide false information or control an algorithm through a black box invasion, the risk would rise even higher. It would be possible to exploit data and mislead its defence mechanisms. The possibility of tricking algorithms through intrusion detection, such as misclassifying an image or supplying inaccurate statistical model, is real and an increasing issue for data security professionals.

CHAPTER 9

WAY FORWARD

A I is not the technology that nations can master working in speculation. A wrong step may lead to humanitarian crises. The technological building-blocks should spread from the private sector to the public sector, from the civilian to the military sphere, between research and industry and between the different strands of AI (complementarity) and countries. The nations should combine together and make the overarching rules that should define the basic parameters and limitation in AI research in the same manner as rules were defined for human cloning.

The assurance of trustworthy, controlled, and responsible AI

Systems containing AI are intended to operate with a certain degree of autonomy. Nevertheless, it is essential for that AI systems designed for militaries must be robust and secure which can be trusted to assist service personnel and commanders, dispelling any "black-box" effect, while retaining human responsibility for action. Trustworthy AI of this sort relies on rigorous systems design which must guarantee total compliance with the human-defined framework.

The human being will then be able to make the most of the system keeping the control with him. The aim is to merge human judgement and algorithmic power to make decisions and function clearly at any time and at a faster rate. Operational performance will then be superior to that of the human being or machine in isolation.

Preserve the resilience and upgradability of systems

Robustness and resilience are critical issues in an environment where the success of engagements depends on communication networks and access to information.

AI-equipped systems will sometimes have to operate in degraded mode in harsh conditions. In such cases, operational units will have to be able to use the systems in that mode and retain the capacity to perform their missions effectively without recourse to AI.

A Robust Framework for The Armed Forces

The Armed Forces are required to be conscious of the ethical and legal issues that may be raised using AI in defence applications, whether for administrative and technical tasks or for operational purposes. Ethics and law are core elements of the service personnel.

To ensure that AI-based technologies do not call these principles into question, especially the place of humans in military action, their development for defence purposes should retain military commanders' responsibility for the use of weapons.

Technical measures to ensure trustworthy AI

AI remains a recent and sometimes immature technology which can generate outputs that humans may perceive as aberrant. Image recognition systems, for example, based on statistical learning and the use of deep neural networks, may produce a completely wrong result, or be duped by a variation of a few pixels. There may be various reasons for these errors:

Errors of implementation, stemming from learning data that are contextualized but not representative of the population as a whole.

Insufficient understanding of the behaviour of the hardware or software integrated into the AI system in relation to the criticality of the job.

The consideration given to AI-related risks in security studies may result in only certain techniques being chosen, according to the criticality of the function.

Govern the data

Having access to reliable, up-to-date data implies exercising control over the data lifecycle from capture to valorisation, including production, processing, and storage. This will be the key issue for the Armed Forces around the globe. It means that data must be regarded as a strategic asset. The twin purposes of data governance are to ensure control of the Strategic assets and to create the climate of trust in which they can be shared, respecting the requirements of regulatory compliance, security, and right use.

Organizations should determine roles and responsibilities for individual handling the data. This involves identifying the actors involved within the scope of the data, defining roles and responsibilities, and organizing the associated cosmetology. Data collection and storage is necessary not only for valorisation but also for successive learning phases. Applications that involve merging and mining distributed data also require substantial telecommunications capacity to limit successive syntheses and fusions which impair the richness of the information contained in the raw data. Once the flow rate is imposed, the optimized distribution of processing will help to ensure that the information contained in the exchanged data is used to best advantage.

Computing power and storage capacity

In addition to data, some applications that use AI require access to very substantial computing power and storage capacity. Cloud computing is one technology that helps to meet those needs. With the cloud, substantial amounts of storage capacity and appropriate computing resources can be allocated very quickly according to needs (a modern jet aircraft, for example, produces 40 terabytes of data per hour).Cloud technology increases infrastructure resilience by quickly and dynamically reallocating resources in the event of a malfunction (if a hard disk fails or a server is lost, for example, environments can be reconstructed rather than repaired).The cloud offers security and reliability. By enabling the automation of actions and the deployment of resources via scripts, it minimizes human intervention and hence the associated risk of error or threat, offering standardization and automation.

CHAPTER 10

CONCLUSION

The latest developments in artificial intelligence is increasingly progressing to the point that it can be used for strategic purposes. The Book discusses AI's potential applications in surveillance, cyber defence and other military applications. AI applications are already taking shape in the real world. More and more autonomous vehicles are being seen in major cities. Moreover, AI has also been implemented in sensor systems, threat assessment systems for air defence, in the analysis of evolving trends in commerce, command and control systems, and smart education applications. However, military AI applications face the following issues which are required to be considered before implementation: -

1. Transparency to ensure that model performance meets military standards.

2. Vulnerabilities that may cause a significant drop in device performance.

Researchers working on AI clarity, interpretability, and ability to explain in a better way have also made significant progress. Many of these advancements are expected to be applied to military AI as well. However, to fully comprehend how this research can be applied, a more detailed requirements review is needed. Military criteria in terms of risk, data quality, legal demands, and so on may be somewhat different, and certain forms of disclosure may not even be relevant. Furthermore, extensive study impact of AI on social values is needed. Future research should focus on how to use the diverse range of visualisation techniques built in the visual analysis field to measure the impact of AI in different fields. Since there is currently no magic solution to the vulnerability issue, it is vital to keep an eye on this field of research and look for promising solutions on a regular basis. However, before such options are accessible, external access to models and defence tactics must be restricted. Otherwise, adversaries may take advantage of the flaws and exploit the weaknesses to their advantage.

The nuclear risk–technological advancement nexus faces challenging as well as urgent problems, including governance concerns. Now is the time for politicians and investors to work with a new generation of players to examine the threats and possibilities of AI applications and to mitigate the former while optimising the latter.

Military AI could eventually displace human responsibility for international security in the far future. While human civilizations do not compete in the conventional sense, mankind may continue to compete with technology to retain the ability to control its own destiny and make independent decisions. Artificial intelligence would increasingly alter the military structures of nations. Military forces are in a process of development of new strike capabilities owing to the rapid advancement in surveillance and command and control technologies. Future wars would be more apt, deadly, unexpected, and volatile because of these war novelties.

To date, humans have willingly assigned tasks to artificial intelligence, which lets them perform their jobs more effectively. Perhaps we are reaching a stage where artificial intelligence will eventually be used to make defence and security decisions as a critical step because finite human capabilities will not give military and political leaders enough time to make thoughtful decisions. Before the future happens, now is the time to make decisions about our planet's secure future—and how far we are going to let AI take over our lives.

LAST THING...

If you enjoyed this book or found it useful I'd be very grateful if you'd post a short review on Amazon. Your support really does make a difference and I read all the reviews personally so I can get your feedback and make this book even better.

Thanks again for your support!

List Of Abbreviations And Acronyms

AI	-	Artificial Intelligence
GPU	-	Graphic processing unit
DL	-	Deep learning
DNN	-	Deep neural Network
NLP	-	Natural language processing
NN	-	Neural Network
IoT	-	Internet of ways
4IR	-	4th Industrial Revolution
ISR	-	Intelligence, Surveillance, and Reconnaissance operation
IBM	-	International business machine
MIT	-	Military Information Technology
ML	-	Machine learning
GAFA	-	Google, Apple, Facebook, Amazon
BATX	-	Baidu, Alibaba, Tencent, and Xiaomi
EU	-	European Union
ICBM	-	Intercontinental Ballistic Missiles
RPA	-	Robotic Process Automation
NPC	-	Nonplaying character

UAV	-	Unmanned Aerial Vehicles
CCW	-	Certain Conventional Weapons
ASAT	-	Anti- satellite
SIOP	-	Single Integrated operational plan
SACCS	-	Strategic Automated Command and control system
DEW	-	Distant early warning line
SAGE	-	Semi-automatic Ground environment
SSBN	-	Nuclear powered ballistic missile
USSR	-	Union of Soviet Socialist Republics
USA	-	United states of America
AIS	-	Automatic identi-fication System
GMM	-	Gaussian Mixture Model
IDS	-	Intrusion Detection System
ATR	-	Automatic target recognition
GAN	-	Generative adversarial network
DARPA	-	Defence Advanced research network
RSS	-	Robotic Surgical Systems
RGP	-	Robotic Ground Platforms

CNAS	-	Centre of new American security
DIU	-	Defence innovation Unit
RMB	-	Renminbi
PLA	-	People's Liberation Army
NSA	-	National Security Agency
BMD	-	Ballistic Missile Defence
ABM	-	Anti-ballistic missile
UUV	-	Unmanned under-water vehicle
DRDO	-	Defence research and development organization
CAIR	-	Centre of Artificial intelligence ad robotics
AINCO	-	AI Net centric operation
UGV	-	Unmanned Group Vehicle
MARF	-	Multi Agent Robotics Framework
LAWS	-	Lethal autonomous weapon system
NORAD	-	North American aerospace Defence command
DOD	-	Department of defence
NC4ISR	-	Nuclear command, control, communication, computer, intelligence, surveillance, and reconnaissance operations

CCIAD   -   Defence artificial Intelligence Coordination unit

Bibliography

Yannis M Assael, Brendan Shillingford, Shimon Whiteson, and Nando de Freitas. Lipnet: End-to-end sentence-level lipreading. GPU Technology Conference, 2017

John Fox, David Glasspool, Dan Grecu, Sanjay Modgil, Matthew South, and Vivek Patkar. Argumentation-based inference and decision making a medical perspective, IEEE intelligent systems, 22(6), 2007

Tianyu Gu, Brendan Dolan-Gavitt, and Siddharth Garg, Badnets: Identifying vulnerabilities in the machine learning model supply chain

Kiian Denos, Mathieu Ravaut, Antoine Fagette, and Hock-Siong Lim, Deep learning applied to underwater mine warfare. In OCEANS 2017-Aberdeen, pages 1–7. IEEE, 2017

Michael Backes, Jorg Hoffmann, Robert Kunnemann, Patrick Speicher, and Marcel Steinmetz, Simulated penetration testing and mitigation analysis

A Tale of Two Cultures: Qualitative and Quantitative Research in the Social Sciences, Gary Goertz James Mahoney

The Russian Military in Contemporary Perspective by Stephen J. Blank Autonomous Weapons and Operational Risk by Paul Scharre

Deep Speech 2: End-to-End Speech Recognition in

English and Mandarin by Dario Amodei, Sundaram Ananthanarayanan, Rishita Anubhai, Jingliang Bai, Eric Battenberg, and Carl Case

Artificial Intelligence, China, Russia, and the Global Order Air University primer [Nicholas Wright, ed. / 2019 / 312 pages / ISBN: 9781585662951 / AU Press Code: B-0161]

An Overview of National AI Strategies by Tim Dutton

Kenneth Payne, Strategy, Evolution, and War: From Apes to Artificial Intelligence (Washington DC: Georgetown University Press, 2018

Artificial Intelligence: A Revolution in Strategic Affairs by Kenneth Payne

The Militarization of Artificial Intelligence by Stanley Center for Peace and Security

Paul Scharre, "Autonomous Weapons and Operational Risk," Center for a New American Security, February 2016

Barry Scott Zellen, State of Doom

Bernard Brodie, the Bomb, and the Birth of the Bipolar World (London: Continuum, 2012)

How artificial intelligence is transforming the world by Darrel M.West and John R.Allen

How Might Artificial Intelligence Affect the risk of Nuclear war by Edward Geist,Andrew

The potential for artificial intelligence in healthcare by Thomas Davenport and Ravi Kalakota

Artificial Intelligence, Transport and the Smart City: Definitions and Dimensions of a New Mobility Era by Alexandros Nikkita's, Kalliopi Michalakopoulou , Eric Tchouamou Njoya

Artificial Intelligence in Games by James Wexler

Yannakakis, Geogios N (2012). "Game AI revisited". Proceedings of the 9th Conference on Computing Frontiers

Artificial Intelligence and its Application in Different Areas by Breaker Heart

https://itchronicles.com/artificial-intelligence/how-do-we-use-ai-in-everyday-life/

https://towardsdatascience.com/how-artificial-intelligence-is-impacting-our-everyday-lives-eae3b63379e1

T. O. Eglington, ``Decision support system"

Geoffrey E. Hinton, Nitish Srivastava, Alex Krizhevsky, Ilya Sutskever, and Ruslan R. Salakhutdinov. Improving neural networks by preventing co-adaptation of feature detectors

Explainable planning by Maria Fox, Derek Long, and Daniele Magazzeni

G. I. Seffers, ``Commanding the future mission, 2016

Cold war lessons for automation in nuclear weapon systems by John Borrie

Anti-satellite Weapons, Deterrence and Sino-American Space Relations by Michael Krepon & Julia

Thompson

Nuclear Early Warning in South Asia: Problems and Issues by M. V. Ramana, R. Rajaraman and Zia Mian

https://www.npr.org/sections/thetwo-way/2016/05/26/479588478/report-u-s-nuclear-system-relies-on-outdated-technology-such-as-floppy-disks

M. Malenic, ``BAE systems wrests air mission-planning development contract from northrop grumman; Defence Daily, vol. 238

Killian Denos, Mathieu Ravaut, Antoine Fagette, and Hock-Siong Lim. Deep learning applied to underwater mine warfare, OCEANS 2017

Gulshan Kumar, Krishan Kumar, and Monika Sachdeva, The use of artificial intelligence-based techniques for intrusion detection: a review. Artificial Intelligence Review

Carlos A Catania and Carlos Garc´ıA Garino, Automatic network intrusion detection: Current techniques and open issues

Robin Sommer and Vern Paxson. Outside the closed world: On using machine learning for network intrusion detection, Security and Privacy (SP), 2010 IEEE Symposium

Artificial Intelligence and National Security, Congressional Research Service

Controlling the development and use of lethal autonomous weapon system by G Bills Geo Wash

New Voices in Grand Strategy

Impact of Industry Innovation Will Continue to Grow at DoD By Cheryl Pellerin

Artificial Intelligence and The Future of Defence, The Hague Centre for Strategic Studies

Autonomy in Russian nuclear forces by Petr Topych-kanov

Early Warning Systems, UNDP

1983 Nuclear False Alarm by Madeline Bradshaw

Overcoming the Abm Treaty: Paths to National Missile Defence by Joseph M. Keenan

Deterrence Instability& Nuclear Weapons in South Asia, STIMSON 2015

Kenneth Waltz, "The Spread of Nuclear Weapons: More May Better," Adelphi Papers

Russia's New Nuclear Weapon Delivery Systems by Franz-Stefan Gady

Artificial Intelligence and Its Impact on the Indian Armed Forces by Maj Gen PK Chakravorty

Luisa M Zintgraf, Taco S Cohen, Tameem Adel, and Max Welling, Visualizing deep neural network decisions: Prediction difference analysis

Jiawei Su, Danilo V. Vargas, and Sakurai Kouichi, One pixel attack for fooling deep neural networks

Anh Nguyen, Jason Yosinski and Jeff Clune, Multi-

faceted feature visualization: Uncovering the different types of features learned by each neuron in deep neural networks
Zachary C Lipton, The mythos of model interpretability 2016

Ian Goodfellow, Jonathon Shlens, and Christian Szegedy. Explaining and harnessing adversarial examples, International Conference on Learning Representations, ICLR, 2015

Papernot, Patrick McDaniel, Somesh Jha, Matt Fredikson, Z. Berkay Celik, and Ananthram Swami, The limitations of deep learning in adversarial settings, IEEE European Sympo- sium on Security & Privacy, 2016

Christian Szegedy, Wojciech Zaremba, Ilya Sutskever, Joan Bruna, Dumitru Erhan, Ian Goodfellow, and Rob Fergus, Intriguing properties of neural networks, International Conference on Learning Representations

Close Calls with Nuclear Weapons, www.ucsusa.org/weaponsincidents

The Impact of Artificial Intelligence on Strategic Stability And Nuclear Risk, Euro-Atlantic Perspectives

Artificial Intelligence and National Security, Congressional Research Service, R45178

Autonomy and Machine Learning as Risk Factors at the Interface of Nuclear Weapons, Computers and People by Avin, Shahar and S.M. Amadae

Sarah Tan, Rich Caruana, Giles Hooker, and Yin Lou, Detecting bias in black-box models using transparent model distillation

Ethic Guideline for Trustworthy, AI High-Level Expert Group on Artificial Intelligence European Commission, B-1049 Brussels

Mobile Autonomous Robot Software (MARS)

C. W. McGee, virtual memory processes and sharing in MULTICS

Autonomous mobile robots in manufacturing: Highway Code development, simulation, and testing by A. Liaqat, W. Hutabarat, L. Tinkler

Man Vs Machine

Twenty years ago, the ultimate man vs machine matchup played out. On one side was humanity's best: Garry Kasparov, arguably the greatest chess player of all time, and the as then world champion. Opposing him was Deep Blue, a chess playing supercomputer built by the engineers at IBM.

By beating Kasparov in the most human pursuit of playing a game of intelligence, chess, Deep Blue ushered AI onto the world stage and into the public's consciousness. Since that day in 1997 debate has raged over the match's significance. Tragedy? Achievement? and it raised a serious question that day "Are we loosing to the machines"

History has very solid examples where automation systems failed, and only human intervention saved the day. The book is an effort to discuss the impacts of Artificial intelligence on command and control systems and how far we are willing to go to forego human control especially at sensitive locations.

ISBN 9798544121985

90000

9 798544 121985